AUTHENTICITY AND GRACE

AUTHENTICITY AND GRACE

Uncovering the Authentic Self

Dr. DAVID T. SMITH

Tampa, Florida

Authenticity and Grace

Published by Gatekeeper Press
7853 Gunn Hwy, Suite 209
Tampa, FL 33626
www.GatekeeperPress.com

Copyright © 2024 Dr. David T. Smith, all rights reserved. No part of this book may be reproduced or transmitted in any form or by any means, electronic or mechanical, including photocopying, recording or by any information storage and retrieval system without written permission from the author.

This publication is designed to provide accurate and authoritative information in regard to the subject matter covered. It is sold with the understanding that the publisher is not engaged in rendering legal or accounting services. If legal advice or other expert assistance is required, the services of a competent professional person should be sought.

ISBN: 9781662955488
eISBN: 9781662955495

Printed in the United States of America

DEDICATION

To the One who has All Power,
to Jessica, and to those who saved
my life; a debt that cannot be repaid
in this lifetime.

CONTENTS

Preface 1

Introduction 5

Part One 9

Part Two 19

Works Cited 35

About the Author 39

PREFACE

It is the morning prayer-walk in spring of the eighth year. At first there was no path. After eight years, you can see a thin line, one worn by rain, wind, boots, and dogs. It winds like a dry creek bed through a tree line, fading through acres of hay and clover, past stacked bee hives, through an apple orchard to a hill top, finally disappearing into the woods and the barbed wire at the property line. The marsh potholes scattered throughout give shelter to nesting ducks, redwing blackbirds, pheasants, deer, muskrat, and fox. Eagles, redtail hawks, and turkey buzzards look down from above while the night gives rise to the floating white and yellow eyes of the now formless deer, fox, possum, and ever deadly coyotes, their purposeful yapping and howling occasionally interrupted by the shrieks of unfortunate rabbits.

We follow the path now by feel. Paced out several times a day, step by step, through scorching heat, pitch blackness, driving rain, blinding and piled snow, through good health and near fatal illness, temperatures ranging between one hundred degrees and thirty below zero. Always for the dogs. Hunting dogs wake up every morning at sunrise; you can feel them watching you, tails drumming the bed, whining, licking, their eyes telling you to "get moving."

The walks started out simple enough, opportunities for meditation and prayer that came out of the never-ending need to run the dogs, eventually evolving into what came to be known as "prayer walks" throughout the day. What started as an admonition became a practice. At some point, through a combination of desperation, perseverance, and Grace, these little walks transformed into an "it." Everything in life that came before was only preparation for the literal "stumbling" across what the twentieth century spiritual leader Emmet Fox called the "Golden Key." What happened next exactly cannot be explained, but can be *related*. It is similar to that state of mind resulting from what Tibetan teacher Chogyam Trungpa calls "meditation in action," a kind of ceaseless awareness opening up from that "nameless place," the one whispered about, but never seen. The timeless certainty coming out of this experience is that we are never alone; we are "undivided" individual expressions of God being itself, all loved, and with a purpose.

This piece "Authenticity and Grace" is

part of the "Orchard Diaries," a collection of essays highlighting methods and techniques for the type of transformative individual freedom people are so desperately searching for today.

INTRODUCTION

THE CHORUS ARISING today from those desiring to live more "authentically," with more "intention," or more "integrity" is a defining feature of our time, the intensity of these yearnings proportionate to the cognitive distortions energizing them. What we refer to as "culture" today is barely more than the sleight of hand produced by a shallow, device-fueled materialism, one that mesmerizes us into believing the ultimate good in life, our "summum bonum," is to be achieved through an endless progression of commodification, control, and consumption. Our lives are spun from the double binding threads shrouding this delusion. Knowing everything about the world, we might control and shape it according to our desires. Conversely, enough control over the world may reveal all of its secrets. But despite our best efforts, while floating upon billowing clouds of meta-data, we stare passively into opaque screens while the entire world is converted into an endless array of consumer products. We dimly sense "something" is off with our perceptions and thinking, a something for which a Google search will not provide a quick and painless solution that Amazon might deliver directly to our door.

Electronic social conditioning is now so powerful that many people confuse the real and virtual worlds. The globalization of technology is negatively affecting humans in a myriad of ways, including through manipulated social contagion, diminished memory, executive function, and attention spans, reduced physical activity, and an epidemic of anxious depression from exposure to prolonged states of "heightened expectancy."[1] Twenty-five years ago, machines were seen as secondary tools for furthering the goals of humanity. In a bizarre reversal, today's techno-oligarchs are converting billions of human beings into extensions of the very machines they used to control. The loss of humanity resulting from this development correlates directly with the increased desire for "authentic living." These yearnings are not benign. They indicate a path through the madness for those with the courage to search it out.

To get beyond mere psychic survival in this technocracy requires us, in the words of Anthony DeMello, to "wake up, and live." Authentic living begins when we jettison the relentless expectations generated by technology-driven desire, fear, and magical thinking. The subsequent absence of these constructs does not produce authenticity. Authenticity is what remains when they disappear. Authenticity is living in the awareness that time and space are simply concepts, the collapse of which reveals the unfolding of the real and eternal present, the "always," wherein "what is is the was of what shall be.[2]" Fully experiencing the present moment occurs when we live in knowledge and awareness of what has traditionally been called "Grace," and living through Grace *is* authentic living. But how and where is it to be found?

PART ONE

IN THE REALM OF THE SPIRIT, it is necessary to distinguish between the world of "words" and the world of "not words." The outer limits of language appear at any attempt to describe the indescribable, as when Van Gogh[3] tried to communicate the horrible suffering of the inhabitants of Montmartre in France, "whose misery one must range among the things that have no name in any language." We can sense the magnitude of their plight, but not much about its true nature. Spiritual phenomena are similar as they exist just beyond our words, detected through perception, awareness, and direct experience. Despite the limitations of language, words can and do provide guiding insights about spiritual phenomena like Grace without necessarily conveying their essence. The sensible approach in these types of explorations is to avoid purely literal or concrete interpretations of words and concepts, especially around esoteric topics. Those who have gone before consistently urge caution as "The words of sages cannot be understood by means of small knowledge, and so the petty man mocks them.[4]"

Cross-cultural descriptions, metaphors, and accounts of the mental states, experiences, and practices surrounding Grace refer to the same basic phenomena. This is confirmed in primary sources such as the Upanishads, the Vedas and Vedanta, the Bhagavad-Gita, the Tao teh Ching, the Dialogues of Plato, the Yogas of Vivekananda, the New Testament and countless other scriptures and spiritual texts anyone can examine. The featured accounts, testimonies, stories, and parables prove beyond doubt there is a "something," *a-life-changing-type-of-knowing* that, upon discovery, transforms people, like the person who, "on finding one pearl of great value, went and sold all that he had and bought it.[5]"

Traditional religions preserve some of their awe and mystery by maintaining the illusion that spiritual ideas and concepts like Grace, or the nature of God, are beyond the scope of the lay population, privy only to the church and its designees. But there exists a monumental spiritual legacy bequeathed to humanity by all the world's luminaries, mystics, rishis, siddhas, sannyasins, and holy people that strikingly proves otherwise. Eknath Easwaran[6] defines mysticism in a way that sweeps aside these ecclesiastic barriers, stating mysticism is simply "the conviction, born of personal experience, that there is a divine core in human personality which each of us can realize directly, and that making this discovery is the real goal of our lives." Accordingly, anyone with this conviction is a potential or actual mystic who has the natural right and capacity to search for and to know this power directly.

Intellectual and scientific pride often discount alternative ways of human knowing beyond those expressed through human thought and language. Sentient beings demonstrate a diverse range in types of knowledge, guidance, and communication, including capacities for echolocation, tidal rhythms, electromagnetic fields, and chemical signaling, most of which are discounted as subhuman "oddities." But human beings have always possessed similar non-cognitive ways of knowing anthropologists indicate have atrophied through the process of civilization, more specifically, urbanization, and that lay dormant but can be re-actualized. It is through the rediscovery and activation of these "thoughtless" ways of knowing that humans can "relearn" to perceive and experience the nature of Grace and other spiritual phenomena. Awakening spiritually involves the development of one's "sixth sense," and Grace is its actuating agent.

The Greek word for Grace is "Charis," which has been defined as "the very energies of God himself... Grace is the working of God himself, not a created substance of any kind that can be treated like a commodity.[7]" And the Hebrew word for Grace is "khen," which translates as "anything that induces a favorable response or something we find ourselves drawn to.[8]" These definitons of Grace indicate it exists *apriori* with a supra-elemental nature, not unlike hydrogen, carbon, or background radiation, it permeates everything, yet is undetectable with the naked eye.

The idea of Grace familiar in Western cultures originates mostly from passages found in Christian religious scriptures, but appears throughout Buddhist, Muslim, Taoist, and other world religions as well. Grace is defined in Christian theology as "the spontaneous, unmerited gift of the divine favor in the salvation of sinners, and the divine influence operating in individuals for their regeneration and sanctification.[9]" Here Grace is viewed as a spirit, energy, or power spontaneously manifesting itself to prevail over sin and evil and can also lead to spiritual growth and transformation. But more important than what Grace can do is *how* Grace works. Grace is freely available, freely given, and has supra-natural regenerative qualities. Individuals living within the conceptual framework of Christianity who report experiencing profound and sometimes inexplicable life changes speak of being "saved" or "reborn" through these powers of Grace.

Grace, on the personal level, is "sensed" in the form of a "beneficent immanent actuality," a type of law, force, power, or energy, with definite qualities like gravity. It exists immanently in each second our "personal reality" unfolds, whether we believe in it, experience it, acknowledge it, or not. This "unmerited gift" is the sum total of spontaneous creation occurring each second to form all that exists and all that may ever come into existence. Grace does not just touch our lives; it *is* our life unfolding instantaneously through time. It is the Alpha and Omega of our individual existence. All life begins when the "gift" of Grace is bestowed, ending when the gift is returned.[10] When you begin to sense the power of this ever-present unfolding, this unearned gift, your life is wondrously changed through *absolutely no effort on your behalf*. This is the inexplicable mystery and paradox of Grace.

Realization of Grace is not dependent on faith or religious affiliation. Anyone in this world, burdened or suffering from loss, poor relationships, addiction, shame, depression, isolation, crisis, and even despair, can learn to see Grace operating in their lives without having any faith in the possibility of it ever happening. It is not true that people require faith to receive Grace. This idea only reinforces their initial suffering by adding the fear of being beyond Grace due to some lack of faith. Belief in the *possibility* of faith can certainly help, but is not required. Under the harshest conditions, when the world and your life are slipping away, something as small as one molecule of belief can snowball to produce a total life transformation. And it can all begin with a perfectly simple belief like this, "It isn't necessary to have something to believe in. It's only necessary to believe that somewhere there's something worthy of belief.[11]"

PART TWO

Learning the signs of Grace and how they appear in our lives begins with understanding simple spiritual principles. Larger questions about whether Grace is granted, given, or earned, or if it bends to personal will, or if it can be influenced by prayer, can be left to the theologians. We are concerned now with developing awareness and perception of our own waypoints to Grace. These markers we can call "Gracepoints." It is our unique Gracepoints that demonstrate the unfolding of Grace in the form of our personal lives. Searching for and discovering our Gracepoints results in different ways of knowing and perceiving reality beyond the limits of the conditioned self. Through bypassing cognition and unwinding some of our conditioned thinking, we begin to dimly perceive that which we have lost, covered over, or buried; the actual experience of the present moment. The highly sought authentic life is simply the freedom and peace resulting from practicing, developing, and experiencing the active presence of Grace unfolding uniquely in the form of your life.

Acknowledgement of the possibility to know Grace in our lives is the starting point for integration, wholeness, and authenticity. It is critically important for spiritual awakening as "the grace of God is the most important factor, because without it, no one would have the fortitude to continue the path leading to God-

Authenticity and Grace

realization. Without the grace of God, no one would have the desire even to begin the search, let alone to pursue the arduous steps which must follow.[12]" Barriers to experiencing Grace arise from the ego and the conditioned self. Though an instinctive tendency exists to fight these elements of the mind, it is not necessary. Gracepoints, by their very nature, indicate clearly and gently which way to go with little or no effort. They demonstrate, in the face of any unfavorable situations or conditions, new ways to observe Grace unfolding in your life today. As Grace unfolds, it activates dormant and atrophied ways of seeing and knowing that transform your vision of the world. We can look at some examples illustrating changes in thinking, attitude, and feeling that occur when you begin your search in earnest.

The starting universal Gracepoint is our deep acknowledgement, understanding, and acceptance that we did not, and do not, create ourselves. Our self and our ego reinforce the delusional belief that we are our own creators. These beliefs present the most formidable barrier to experiencing the unfolding of Grace as our reality. Current neuroscience and quantum physics are now laughably, converging on the "discovery" that human consciousness "unfolds" each moment of our lives to appear in the form of our lives. Ironically, this had not only been experienced, documented, and communicated thousands of years ago in the Vedas and Vedanta, but also confirmed by the luminaries who followed like Buddha, Lao Tzu, and Jesus of Nazareth. Science and spirituality agree now that the human mind creates individual yet similar versions of the world by converting sensory input generated by perception into a type of collective "hallucination" unique to our species.

What the mystics have referred to as the "Void," or the "Way," and what Christians call the "Father within," or what we call "Reality," or "God," are the words that represent the moment to moment unfolding of an eternal "immanence" appearing in the form of our world and our individual lives in a process of unceasing spontaneous creation. The actuation or manifestation of *our* specific existence from out of this ever-present potentiality is signified by the word Grace. The actual "gift" of Grace referred to in spiritual texts is the fact that each moment unfolds in our specific "*this*" instead of a different "*that*." If reality unfolded any other way, we would not exist. It appears, at least momentarily, that Grace has chosen us.

Understanding the nature, power, and breadth of this constant and specific gift to each of us, this "revelation of immanence," results in the necessary destruction of the self-centered mind and its erroneous beliefs about the "self" that obscure our true awareness of the nature of reality. As unreal and unnecessary beliefs fall away, our minds rearrange, creating new spaces and awakening dormant capacities and new possibilities for knowing. Watching and feeling how existence is created in each unfolding second out of all immanent potential possibilities, is to witness how it is that "From wonder into wonder Existence opens.[13]"

Spiritual writers in the tradition of Alan Watts and Joel Goldsmith provide our second Gracepoint. To paraphrase Watts, we do not come *in* to this world, we are born *out* of it, or created *from* it. We are told we come in to this world, as if from some other place and made of different material. But we are created through the same process which creates everything else. We are part of "it," and "it" is part of us. When conditioned belief in our "otherness" collides with our natural instincts, it produces the tension driven feelings of separateness from the world around us, the same ones providing the ego its lifelong opportunities for defiance. And without being aware of it, this is the situation most people try and escape their entire lives, grasping for the straws that only reinforce this splitting tension within themselves.

Goldsmith clarifies this dilemma by pointing out there is not a God, a world, and us, but that God is actually *being* us. As he explains, "God is working out Its life as our life. God is individual life. God is working out Its life in what appears to be the form of our lives. God is working out Its life as our individual consciousness. God is working out Its plan in us and through us. In this knowledge we relax and become beholders. It is no longer our life: It is God's life unfolding individually. God appears on earth as individual you and me, and as we step aside, we begin to see God shining through.[14]" Watts would always humorously reinforce this same point by stating humans are simply an example of God "peopling" itself.

Vivekananda's essays on Karma Yoga, the Yoga of work, provide us Gracepoint three. Throughout this series, he explains the benefit of the deliberate practice of non-attachment from all our work and activity. Detachment is not to be confused with the negation associated with religious practices involving renunciation, self-mortification, or self-denial. Detachment is a mental practice, an act of will and choice, that over time shows us how we play our part in the vast and momentary unfolding of creation. As we learn to detach, our perceptual vantage point shifts from the egocentric "I" position, to a more peripheral viewpoint from which we can now see we do not create, nor are we responsible for reality. We become participant observers in and of it. When this perceptual shifting begins, the ego begins its fight for self-preservation. This is precisely the point we reinforce our practice of detachment to protect and free ourselves from the conditioned self.

The "I" we think we are is relentlessly conditioned to "get ahead," and to "push forward," and "accomplish and succeed." We are told, "the world is yours for the taking." This process creates the all-powerful "self" that stands in opposition to reality. We watch ourselves proclaim "I did this!" and "I did that!" When we begin to see through this illusion, the ego throws up a wall of doubt and fear, our complicit defense mechanisms desperately arranging resistances ranging from ego maniacal grandiosity, somatization, and mental illness, to complete self-destruction. This pathological protection of the false sense of oneself is what in extreme forms creates the aberrant traits of tyrants, predators, bureaucrats, propagandists, and sociopaths. The ego is always parasitic in this way, corrupting every human dignity to preserve itself without killing off its host completely.

Awareness of Grace removes the need to fight the conditioned self. Learning through our work to concentrate task by task, regardless of how menial, moving on each moment without thought of how it will benefit us or affect the world, leads us to a detachment that transmutes our work into pure action. Through this practice, the idea of the self as creator of everything begins to fall away and work is no longer tiring or burdensome. It becomes more of an act of love, not in oneself anymore, but in reality, and action. Paradoxically, we prevail over our lower selves by working through the false ideas about the self and the fruits of its actions.

Vivekananda[15] instructs us that "To attain this unattachment is almost a life-work, but as soon as we have reached this point, we have attained the goal of love and become free; the bondage of nature falls from us, and we see nature as she is; she forges no more chains for us; we stand entirely free and take not the results of work into consideration; who then cares for what the results may be?" For every outcome of our prior work, we can now see that in each and every case, *someone* or *something* opened the space we filled through our original efforts. We believe we push forward and "make things happen," when we really are gently and always being pulled forward by Grace. No work has ever been accomplished through our efforts alone. This realization helps reduce the massive outlay of ego sustaining energy that prevents us from living in the present and sets us free. It also makes us more creative and our work becomes attractive and fulfilling once again.

The fourth Gracepoint involves the realization that we always have unfailing knowledge of the "correct" thing to do in every life situation. If you review every mistake in your life, you will see that in every case without fail, if only for a microsecond, you had knowledge of the correct thing to do at that time. This ever-present knowledge of the correct thing to do at all times is the manifestation of the "Grace of God." This is like a human superpower. Unfortunately, true to our human nature, having this knowledge does not mean we act correctly in each and every case. While we are given the gift of knowledge of the correct thing to do, it is always accompanied by our free will. When we realize that we have always had this knowledge then continue to make mistakes, we begin to grow up and no longer project the blame onto those around us, the system, the world, or God. We begin to accept responsibility for our decisions and mistakes and make better choices with our free will moving forward.

The fifth and last Gracepoint involves developing a comprehensive "letting go" of our conditioned thinking and its resultant behavior. We are trained to believe that letting go of ideas, thinking, and behavior, no matter how ineffective or problematic, constitutes a type of quitting, failure, or weakness, a kind of last-ditch surrender. We hold on until we are forced to let go and then only glumly or reluctantly. This type of passive or resistant letting go appears at times only to turn people into angry "doormats." This is not a true letting go, but only a child's resistant quitting or actual giving up. It often results in a doubling down on remaining resistances in a kind of "I'll show you" attitude. There is a tidal difference between the spirit of quitting and that of deliberately letting certain things go. Quitting only preserves darkness and continues to drain life energy meant for greater things while keeping us slaves to circumstance. This type of stubborn denial and ignorance creates a barrier, inhibiting the natural flow of Grace that sustains spiritual growth and development.

True letting go is an active and dynamic process requiring humility, discipline, intelligence, and willpower. Awareness of Grace provides the energy, insight, and clarity needed for us to let go and detach from that which we no longer need. Vivekananda[16] indicates one way many achieve this goal, "It is a most difficult thing to give up the clinging to this universe; few ever attain to that... The vast majority of mankind choose... the way through the world, making use of all the bondages themselves to break those very bondages. This is also a kind of giving up; only it is done slowly and gradually, by knowing things, enjoying things, and thus obtaining experience, and knowing the nature of things until the mind lets them all go at last and becomes unattached."

This Eastern practice and achievement of the letting go of old ideas and behaviors is not unlike the ancient practice of the "philosophical life." Plato, through the personae of Socrates, tells us how it is that "Ordinary people seem not to realize that those who really apply themselves in the right way to philosophy are directly and of their own accord preparing themselves for dying and death.[17]" Plato is not here referring to physical death, but to the metaphorical "dying unto self" mentioned in all spiritual traditions, leading to the life of the spirit through awareness of Grace. This moving beyond one's self can be achieved, at least partially, through discovery and application of any particular Gracepoints that move us away from the tyranny of the self toward true freedom, the real summum bonum (ultimate good) of our lives.

In the end, awareness of Grace allows us to avoid the tragic mistake of confusing the trappings of material success and comfort with those of enlightenment. Breaking from the illusory and virtual worlds, we return at once to the one and only world that *is*. Few are those who, testing the limits of language and passing beyond the prison walls of the conditioned self, come to *know* their lives as the activity of Grace unfolding. This is the place at the center of our being, where, after all the distractions have run their course and fallen away, we truly grow in spirit and character and become who we were meant to be. Paradoxically, it is discovering, or more accurately, uncovering the unreal nature of the self that gives us a glimpse of reality as it *is*. If through the power of Grace this awakening occurs, we do not stop living, but we live anew; we are no longer burdened and ensnared by the world and its people. We are free to the extent we invite and allow Grace to dissolve barriers between ourselves and reality, uncovering the buried places within where things become possible once again. This is the foundation for authentic living.

WORKS CITED

1. Kramer, et. al. (2014). Experimental Evidence of Massive-scale Emotional Contagion Through Social Networks. *Proceedings of the National Academy of Sciences of the United States of America, III*, pp. 8788-90. Retrieved July 14, 2024, from https://doi.org/10.1073/pnas.1320040111

2. Bynner, W. (1986). *The Way of Life According to Lao Tzu*. W. Bynner, Trans., p. 32. Putnam.

3. Van Gogh, V. (2023). *Dear Theo*. Kindle Edition ed., p. 38. Grapevine India Publishers.

4. Confucius. (n.d.). *The Analects*. Kindle Edition ed., p. 348. Penguin Group, USA.

5. Nelson, T. (1982). *Holy Bible*. p. 1128. Harper Collins Christian Publishing.

6. Easwaran, E. *Conquest of Mind*. Kindle Edition, p. 4.

7. OrthodoxWiki. (2011, April 19). Grace. Retrieved July 13, 2024, from https://orthodoxwiki.org/index.php?title=Grace&oldid=100098

8. Biblical Scholar Team. (2020, September 18). *Kehn: What is the Definition of Grace?* Retrieved from BibleProject Scholar: https://bibleproject.com/articles/biblical-grace-and-a-generous-god/

9. Britannica, T. E. (2023, April 7). https://www.britannica.com/topic/grace-religion.

10. Epictitus. (1998). *Discourses* (Vol. 1). (W. Oldfather, Trans.) Harvard University Press.

11. Bester, A. (1956). *The Stars My Destination*. p. 270. Boylston & Company, Publishers.

12. Goldsmith, J. (1956). *The Art of Meditation* (Kindle ed.) p. 7. Longboat Key: Acropolis Books.

13. Bynner, W. (1986). The Way of Life According to Lao Tzu. W. Bynner, Trans., p. 1. Putnam.

14. Goldsmith, J. (1958). *Practicing the Presence* (Kindle ed.) pp. 28-9. Longboat Key, FL, USA: Acropolis Books.

15. Vivekananda. (1953). *The Yogas and Other Works* (Kindle ed.) p. 35. New York: Ramakrishna-Vivekananda Center.

16. Vivekananda. (1953). The Yogas and Other Works (Kindle ed.) p. 54. New York: Ramakrishna-Vivekananda Center.

17. Plato. (1961). *The Collected Dialogues.* (E. Hamilton, & H. Cairns, Eds.) p. 47. Princeton University Press.

ABOUT THE AUTHOR

David T. Smith, PhD received honors in philosophy from New York University before working in public and private sector healthcare, eventually holding professorships in Community and Clinical Psychology. Dr. Smith has published applied research in healthcare on healing factors, technology, and patient outcomes. His scholarly interests focus on the philosophical, psychological, and spiritual needs of the individual in modern society. He is currently a personal consultant living with his family in rural America.

www.ingramcontent.com/pod-product-compliance
Lightning Source LLC
LaVergne TN
LVHW011900060526
838200LV00054B/4447